In My Preschool

In My Preschool

There is a Time for EVERYTHING

Sylvia A. Rouss

A Dragonfeather Book
Bedazzled Ink Publishing Company * Fairfield, California

978-1-960373-06-9 paperback

Cover Photo
by
C.A. Casey

Cover Design
by

Photos taken by
C.A. Casey
Claudia Wilde
Jessie Kirchhoff
of the Pre-K Class
Anna Kyle Elementary School, Fairfield, California

Dragonfeather Books
a division of
Bedazzled Ink Publishing Company
Fairfield, California
http://www.bedazzledink.com

In my preschool
there is a time for everything.

There is a time for family . . .

and a time
for friends.

There is a time to learn . . .

and a
time to
play.

Then, there is a time to talk . . .

and a time to listen.

Often there is
a time
for noise . . .

and sometimes
a time
for quiet.

There is also a time

to be messy . . .

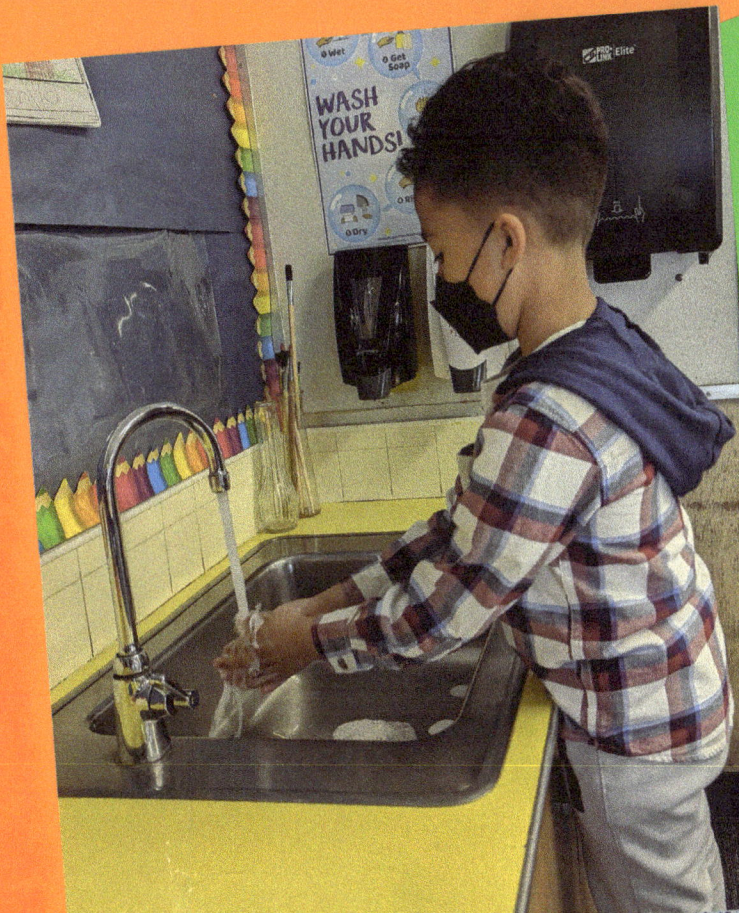

and
a
time

to
be
clean.

There is a time for walking . . .

and even times for running.

Sometimes,
there is time for sadness . . .

but always a time to be happy.

We have lots of time
to be together . . .

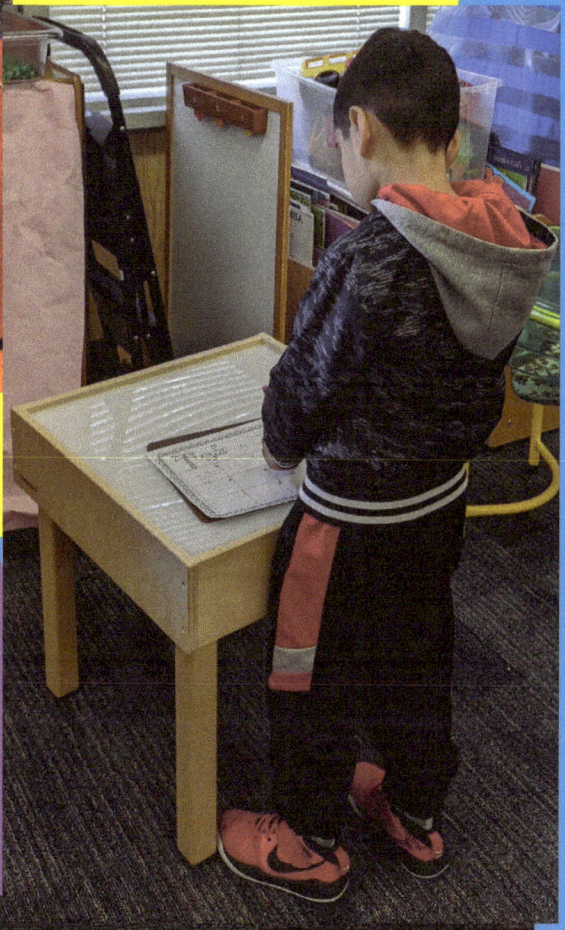

and even
times to be
by ourselves.

At lunch, there is a time for our meal . . .

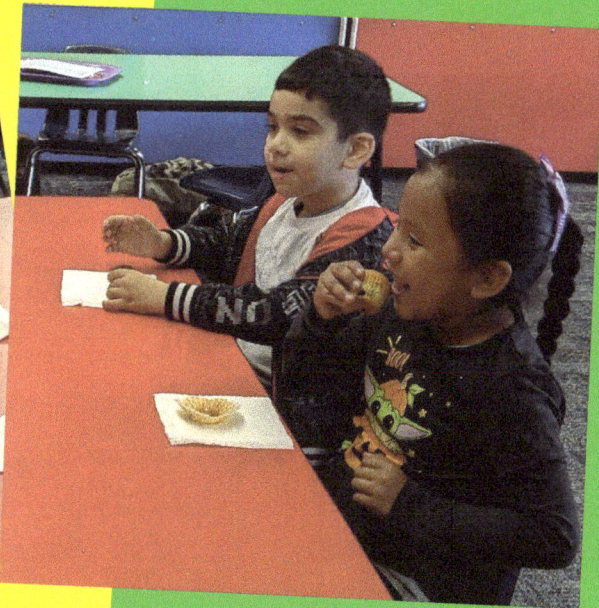

and on special occasions,
a time
for dessert.

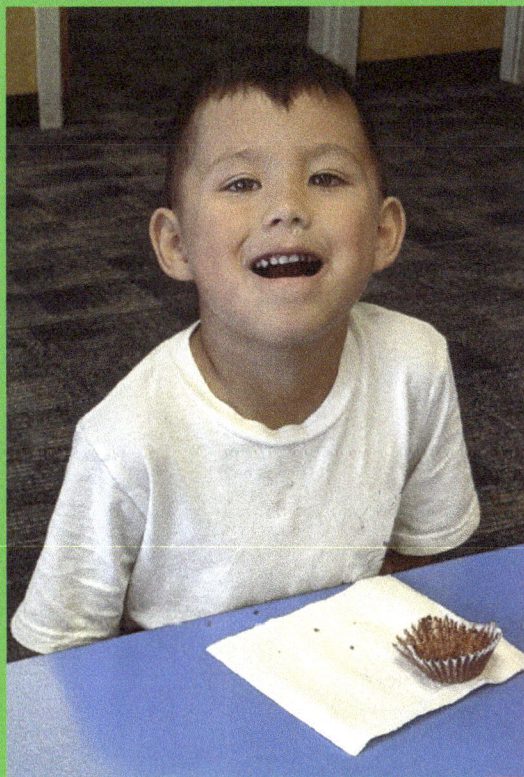

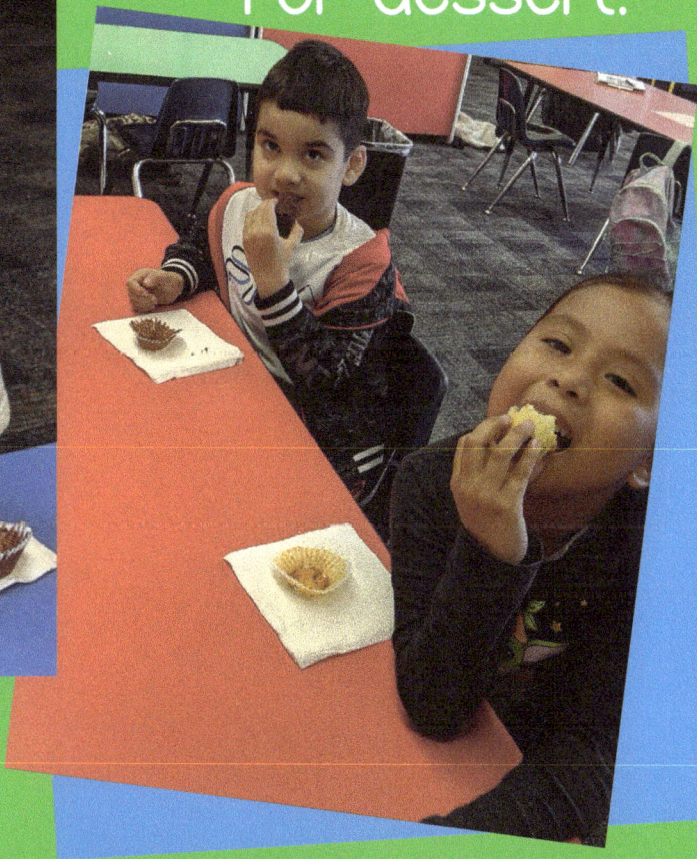

During the day,
there is a time to rest . . .

and a time to wake up.

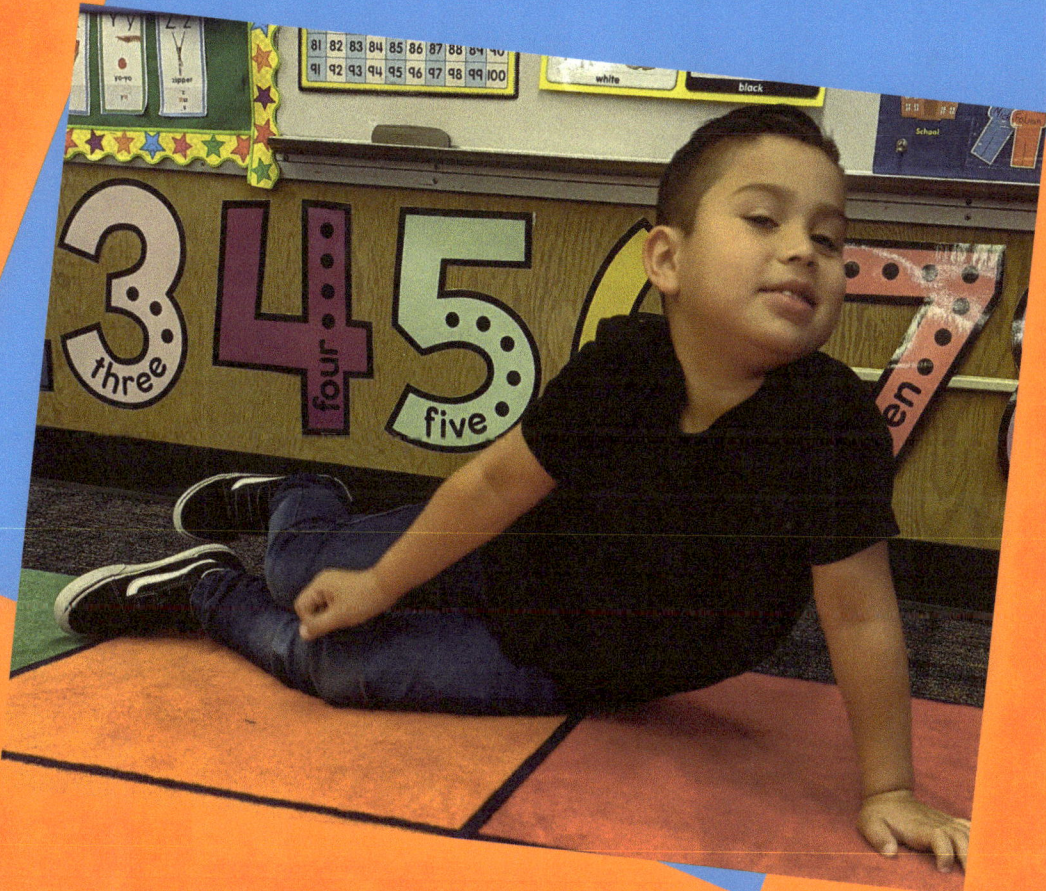

When my school day is over,
there is a time to say goodbye.

There is a time
for everything
in my preschool.

Thank you!

Mrs. Jessie Kirchhoff and her awesome Pre-K Class
Anna Kyle Elementary School, Fairfield, California

NOTE TO PARENTS AND TEACHERS

As a college student, I loved the power and beauty of the Byrds' interpretation of the Pete Seeger song "Turn! Turn! Turn!" When I learned that the song was based on the Biblical verses of Ecclesiastes, and that it's essential meaning is that there is "plan for everything, but a plan that we may not always understand," I was both enthralled and challenged. The poetry of this Old Testament chapter had been read and sung in prayers and hymns for centuries by both Jews and Christians.

I hope that my retelling of Ecclesiastes keeps the beauty of the traditional cadence and the power of the text's symmetry but uses concepts that are age appropriate for young children, with verses that mirror the school day for a preschooler.

This book is intended to be an introduction to preschool. The words and photographs in this book depict the range of the activities and experiences of a typical preschool day. And while most preschools have similar routines, each child's experiences are unique. Because while children are developing intellectually, they are also developing socially and emotionally at their own pace. A normal school day is full of learning activities but at the same time, children are learning to navigate the intricacies of social relationships and coping with emotions. During a school day, children may take joy in learning and making friends but sometimes they might feel angry or sad and those feelings are okay too. Hopefully children will find this book engaging and give parents and teachers opportunities for discussion.

Sylvia Rouss grew up in California and first began writing for the children in her preschool class. As an early childhood educator, she was the recipient of the Samuel Glasner Creative Teaching Award and the Grinspoon Steinhardt Award for excellence in Jewish education. Sylvia credits the children in her classroom for her inspiration. She is the author of more than 50 published books including the *Sammy Spider* series, as well as *The Littlest* series. She received the National Jewish book Award for her story, *The Littlest Pair* and she received the Sydney Taylor Honor Award for *Sammy Spider's First Trip to Israel* and *Mitzvah the Mutt*. *Sammy Spider's First Shavuot* and *Tali's Jerusalem Scrapbook* were named Sydney Taylor Notable Books. Sylvia resides in Oxnard with her husband, Jeff, and has three married adult children and seven grandchildren. Besides family and writing, she maintains a busy schedule that includes lecturing and book readings throughout the United States, Europe and Israel. Her stories have been translated into Spanish, Dutch, French and Portuguese.

www.ingramcontent.com/pod-product-compliance
Lightning Source LLC
LaVergne TN
LVHW070839080426
835512LV00025B/3484